DON'T DIE SITTING WORKBOOK

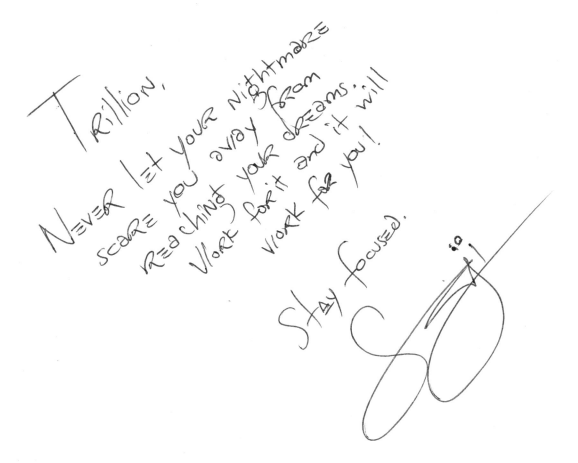

Trillion,

Never let your nightmare scare you away from reaching your dreams. Work for it and it will work for you!

Stay focused.

"The person who risks nothing,
does nothing, has nothing,
is nothing, and will be nothing."

— Leo Buscaglia

DON'T DIE SITTING WORKBOOK

SAJI IJIYEMI

BALTIMORE   LAGOS   BRUSSELS

Published in the USA by
Mastars Media. *A Mastars Group LLC Company*
P. O. Box 22927, Baltimore, MD 21203.

ISBN: 978-0-9839541-3-2
Library of Congress Control Number: 2011963661
1. Christian Living 2. Inspirational 3. Personal Development.

Edited by Miranda Ijiyemi and Douglas Russell
Cover and interior design by Saji Ijiyemi/Mastars Media
Cover photo credit: © Istockphoto / Rubberball

Printed in the United States of America.

CONTENTS

HOW TO USE THIS WORKBOOK

In my experience, I learn best when I recognize what I need to do instead of writing down what I am reading or hearing. When answering the questions in this workbook, I encourage you to write down what you will do, and if possible, when you will do it because you are more likely to apply what you have learned if you take time to write down your own thoughts, plan of action, and conclusions. Unfortunately, many books do not have a workbook and only provide information without application, knowledge without wisdom, and inspiration without action.

What will you do differently as a result of the new information you have learned from reading *Don't Die Sitting*? Did you even take time to write down your thoughts or plan of action? Since this is where most people fail, this interactive workbook is designed to not only help you capture your thoughts but also help you cement and practice them. It might take a bit of time for you to answer some of the questions, but that is perfectly okay. So, don't rush! There is no right or wrong answer. This exercise is about your life, and only you know what you need to do to live more effectively.

I'm sure you are willing to change your life. Unlike most people who have read *Don't Die Sitting* but didn't consider getting the workbook to reflect on the lessons learned and applying the new information, you took the time to reflect, rethink, and redirect your life. If this workbook does not provide enough space for you to write, I encourage you to get a journal and continue to process your thoughts and ideas there. If you are going to make your days count instead of counting your days, you will have to create the time to act on the thoughts you will capture in this workbook and see your life change.

Getting this workbook represents only 5 percent of the effort; taking the time to answer the questions accounts for 15 percent, and the remaining 80 percent involves the discipline needed to taking action every day and doing something you promised to do. You have greatness in you. Just *Don't Die Sitting* on it.

—Saji Ijiyemi
Baltimore, MD, USA.

FOREWORD

The *Don't Die Sitting* workbook will be a great resource to many. Whether you choose to use it for a small group, a Bible study class, Bible college students, or your own personal study, you will find it very inspirational. The casual reader will find this workbook both stimulating and thought provoking. *Don't Die Sitting: The Workbook*, along with the book, will challenge and motivate you to go to the next level.

Saji Ijiyemi's reasearch for both the book and workbook is thorough, informative, and powerful. The direct quotes found in the book will spiritually enlighten and encourage you. The workbook will further challenge your spiritual development. It will help move you from sitting on the sidelines of life to positioning you for your God-ordained destiny. I trust that this workbook will help move you from the average and mundane to superseding the average. It will help you understand your personal limitations while highlighting your unique strengths.

We have been eagerly awaiting the release of this workbook. Our church is planning on using this for our Bible study class. I highly recommend other leaders to do the same. In the words of Saji Ijiyemi, "Nothing is worse than doing nothing."

Enjoy the challenge in the pages to come!

—Lewis Lee
Senior Pastor, Life Source Revival Center
Baltimore, MD.

A NOTE FROM SAJI

"Think on these things"

Mobile technology has changed and is still changing our life in so many ways. We can hardly walk or talk without our mobile phones. Its alarm wakes us up, its beeping alerts us, and according to 2014 Pew Research, 67 percent of mobile phone owners find themselves checking their phone for messages, alerts, or calls—even when they don't notice their phone ringing or vibrating. Forty-four percent have slept with their phone next to their bed, and 29 percent describe their mobile phone as "something they can't imagine living without."

Picking up our mobile phone has taken priority over both Morning Prayer and morning coffee. From dusk to dawn, we are constantly bombarded with information. With close to two billion smartphone users worldwide and the touch of a screen, we can now connect everywhere, with everyone and everything—except ourselves. We have disconnected with ourselves in an attempt to be connected with the world.

In today's world where we leave a screen at home, drive with a screen in the car, work on another screen on the job, only to come back to the first screen we left at home, it is becoming increasingly difficult to set some time aside for ourselves—to be free from distractions and be able to examine, meditate, and reflect on our life and priorities.

I have received phone calls, emails, social media messages, and testimonies of how **Don't Die Sitting** has inspired many people to take action, but they don't know how or where to get started. If you've been asking a similar question, this workbook is your answer.

More than a million books are published every year in the U.S. alone, but if just proliferation of knowledge makes life any better, so many lives would have been transformed by now. It does not matter how many books you read in a day if you do not take time to reflect, think, and cement your learning with action.

I encourage you to take some time out of your busy schedule to reflect on the questions in this workbook and record your thoughts in the space provided. You might want to turn off the mobile phone, find a place without any distractions, and examine your life. As the Greek philosopher Socrates said, "The unexamined life is not worth living." I pray that you will not live that kind of life.

INTRODUCTION

*Before you begin: Please familiarize yourself with the **Introduction** to Don't Die Sitting, pp. 15–20.*

Don't Die Sitting was inspired by people who have not allowed their disability to affect their ability. The heroes and "sheroes" you read about in the book have found hope in their hopeless situations and successfully taken advantage of their disadvantages.

What would you do differently if you were to lose one or both of your arms or legs or they become disabled?

_____

_____

_____

If you currently have any form of (physical) disability, how has this condition affected what you want to do in life?

_____

_____

_____

Physically challenged celebrities such as Stevie Wonder, Nick Vujicic, Natalie du Toit, and Yinka Ayefele have not allowed their disability to limit their ability. Do you think they are just lucky?

_____

_____

_____

Part One — Challenges

Do you feel your race, color, background, and/or nationality affect your success in life?

_____

_____

_____

Part Two — Chances

Do you think other people who are successful in life have more opportunities than you?

_____

_____

_____

Part Three — Choices

Will you agree that you are where you are today because of the choices you have made in the past or because of fate?

_____

_____

_____

Part Four — Changes

What one thing do you think has to change for everything to change for the better for you?

_____

_____

_____

PART ONE

Challenges

You are not alone

DIFFICULT TIMES

If you faint in the day of adversity, your strength is small.

If you give up when trouble comes, it shows that you are weak.

*Before you begin: Please familiarize yourself with **Chapter 1** of Don't Die Sitting, pp. 23–31.*

No matter who you are or what you have, you will face difficult times. Problems are signs that you are still alive. You probably know that place you get to where you have no problems at all—it's called the grave, and nobody wants to go there. Good things do happen to bad people, and bad things happen to good people. It's just life. There are graduates who are broke, while dropouts legitimately make millions of dollars. There are good, honest, and religious people who are battling sickness, while dishonest, bad, and irreligious people are healthy. There are loving, caring, and dedicated couples who have no children, while those who are blessed to have them are looking for ways to abort. There are gifted people who are stuck and suffering from depression, while people who are not any better than they are advance and enjoy life.

You may ask, "Why is life so difficult at times?" "Why am I not seeing any progress even when I'm doing everything I know to do?" "Why all these troubles?" "Why me?" If you've been asking these kinds of questions, you are not alone.

1.1 We All Have Challenges

In 2004, I arrived in the USA with a diplomatic visa because my wife, at that time, was working for the Netherlands Embassy in Washington, D.C. As you can imagine, life was good. In August 2006, my wife was transferred back to Europe, and my diplomatic visa expired two months later. I lost my job as a federal contractor. I could not get an employer to file for a work visa on my behalf, and I didn't have a place I could call home. I could not see my then four-month-old daughter because she went with my wife to Europe. I was driving through town with an expired diplomatic license plate. I didn't have any income, and I was living in my car. I woke up one morning that October 2006 and discovered that I was broke, homeless, unemployed, separated from my family, and an illegal alien in the USA—those were difficult times!

It did not take me long to realize, however, that I was not the only one without legal status in the USA. At that time, there were about six million illegal immigrants in the USA, most of whom were broke, unemployed or illegally employed with a fake identity, separated from their families, driving without a driver's license, homeless, helpless, and penniless. When I realized that I was not the only one with immigration issues, I was a little comforted and confident that my situation would change for the better one day—especially when I heard that someone had just obtained their legal immigration papers.

What are you going through right now? What are the BIGGEST challenges you are facing right now? Identify them and list them. Let it all out! You can overcome them. You can get out of them, but you first have to acknowledge them. Ignoring your challenges will not make them go away. Go ahead and list them

_____

_____

_____

_____

_____

_____

1.2   You Can Prepare For Difficult Times

"If you keep living, difficult times will come."

During the 2008 economic recession, many people lost their homes to foreclosure, some lost their jobs, family income decreased, and real estate lost value. Businesses were shut down, spending dropped, and debt rose. I don't know if you lost anything during the recession, but I lost my house, and I'm glad I did not lose my life. Several years after the recession, many survivors are still dealing with episodes of fear, low self-esteem, anxiety, and depression. I experienced all these negative emotions when it seemed that I had lost everything, but one thing that kept me sane was my mother's advice. Mom always says, "There is nothing to fear if the sky is going to fall because you are not the only one under it." As I grew, I discovered that troubles are everywhere; everybody may experience the same storm, but we all respond differently based on our perspective and our preparation. You prepare for war in times of peace, but, unfortunately, we sometimes forget that life is a battle. We let down our guard and are surprised again by problems.

Looking at challenges you listed in 1.1 above, have you ever thought of how you will respond to them before they happened?

_____

_____

_____

Have you ever thought about the next step you would take if you were let go from your job next week? How would you respond if your spouse decided, without any fault on your side, that he or she is leaving you? What would you do if you lose all your savings? "But, Saji, all these things are negative thinking," you say. I don't call it negative thinking though. I call it life, and these things happen to good and bad people. Now write down what you would do with all the problems you listed in 1.1 above. How could you begin to respond instead of reacting to them? Write down the steps you would take tomorrow, next week, or next month.

_____

_____

_____

_____

_____

_____

If you look at your life and conclude these are difficult times, you have to believe there is hope and you will win if you don't quit. If things are going well for you right now, congratulations! But be prepared, because if you keep living, difficult times will come.

1.3   Know Where Your Help Comes From

"The best of men are still men at their very best."

If you are frustrated and angry with life right now, I can guess that people have disappointed you or things have not turned out the way you expected. I understand that people have promised to do something, but they have refused to come through on their promises. But for how long are you going to be angry? Men and women can fail you, and they will fail you, which is why it is important to know where you can get help. When things were tough in Samaria, a woman put her trust in the government, but the government failed her. When the time came for me to start my career as a college graduate, I put my trust in a man, but he died when I needed him most. So take time to reflect on where you expect help to come from.

Considering the challenges you might be facing right now and the help you badly need—money, family, immigration issues, your job, relationships, your health, negative emotions—where do you expect help to come from?

Who do you think will help you? Why?

What is your plan B if (or when) the person or the institution you are counting on fails?

When you are in serious difficulties and no one seems available to help you, you have to know what to do. King David said, "My help comes from the God who made the heavens and the earth." God can use people to help you, but it is safer to put your trust in God, not in people.

1.4   Don't Let Fear Stop You

"There is nothing to fear but fear itself."

— *Franklin D. Roosevelt*

Because of their fear of the Syrian army, the residents of Samaria had become prisoners in their own city. The dread of the Syrian army had locked them up, both physically and emotionally, and they dared not venture out of the city. It is true that life sometimes happens to you, but you can also be intimidated, frustrated, and stuck if you are afraid to take a bold, actionable step toward your goal in life. Is it possible that you are not on the way to a successful life because you are in the way? Your potential, your gifts, and your talents are in danger of being lost forever if you let fear stop you.

Is it possible that you are not any further than you are right now because you fear what might happen or what someone will say or think? Take some time to reflect on a major step you want to take or a major decision you want to make. Instead of thinking about what might happen if you make that move, write down what might happen if you don't:

_____

_____

_____

_____

_____

_____

Let's assume you have the assurance that you are not going to fail, and that you are guaranteed to win, what will you start doing right away?

_____

_____

_____

Listen! Nothing out there has enough power to stop you; all that is keeping you from taking that courageous step into your future is your imagination and the fear of what might or might not happen. But if you do nothing, time will soon run out and you will die—sitting on your potential. If you allow fear to stop you, you will end up a prisoner of your own fear, and the enemy will use what you fear to shut you out of your destiny. Don't put yourself behind bars; break the chain of fear and declare your freedom.

1.5   See an Opportunity

"We often miss opportunity because it's dressed in overalls and looks like work."

— *Thomas Edison*

The U.S. federal government has a website called FedBizOpps that lists problems the government wants to solve. Those who actually make money from the opportunities, however, are those who are prepared to solve the problems that come with the published opportunities. What you are crying about right now just might be an opportunity. What you are complaining about right now might also be another opportunity. Every problem you face is actually an opportunity; it all depends on what you see. If you don't want to die with your dream locked up inside you, you need to summon courage to step out of the comfort boat of familiarity to walk on the waters of uncertainty. You've got to be willing to leave what is not working, who is not working, and those who are not walking so that you can check out the opportunity in front of you. .

> *You've identified your BIGGEST challenges, you've listed how you are going to take them on, you've recognized where your help comes from, and you've resolved that fear will not stop you. To handle life's difficult situations with grace, you need to change the way you look at your problems. This will cause a shift in your thinking process, and it can change your life for good. Peter took advantage of the storm, the wind, and the waves to walk on the same water he should have sank in. He saw an opportunity in time of trouble. Now review all the challenges and the problems you listed in 1.1. above, and list the opportunities you can seee:*

_____
_____
_____
_____
_____
_____

Your ~~problem~~ opportunity is calling you to a new dimension, but fear is holding you back. Step out of your current comfort zone and try something new. Even if you fail, you might make history in the process.

Now that you know what to do in difficult times, let's talk about the attitude that is needed when life gets really tough. .

POSITIVE ATTITUDE

Use the power of your tongue, don't abuse it.

*Before you begin: Please familiarize yourself with **Chapter 2** of Don't Die Sitting, pp. 33–41.*

I f your life has not turn out the way you expected, take stock of your actions and decisions before now, evaluate them, and take responsibility for how you got here and how you intend to get there. Blaming your parents, your community, your church, or your government will not make you any better. You can survive whatever you are going through right now if you accept total responsibility for your life and have a positive attitude.

2.1   Don't Blame Others, Take Absolute Responsibility

"If you want to get ahead in life, you must learn to accept responsibility."

If you want to maximize your potential and not die—sitting on your talents, you must accept total and absolute responsibility for where you are and what you have right now. You must accept that you are where you are right now because of you and nobody else. You cannot change what you avoid and you will not change as long as you still have one more person or one more situation to blame. If your life is not going the way you want, take some time to reflect on the actions you have taken and the decisions you have made that might have brought you to this point.

Can you identify any action or decision that might have brought you to your current unpleasant situation? As you complete this section, think of the opportunities you have missed, the time and resources you have wasted on purposeless activities, or the poor financial decisions you have made. Reflect on the bad, negative, and unhealthy relationships you have committed yourself to, and consider your unhealthy food and exercise habits. It might even be laziness, procrastination, passivity, or lackadaisical attitude. What will you take absolute responsibility for doing?

_____

_____

_____

_____

_____

_____

2.2   Stay Calm

"No matter what you are going through, be patient and be determined that your problem will not see your end and that you will see the end of your problem."

Like a furnace reveals what gold is made of, the real you will show up in times of crisis. The city of Samaria was hit with a military invasion, an economic downturn, and food scarcity. The situation brought out the best in some and the worst in others. The true leader of the city emerged in crisis. In contrast to the king's erratic behavior, the prophet was calming, encouraging, and assuring the city elders that the present trouble would not last long. In the midst of trouble, the prophet was relaxed, composed, and positive because he knew that God is a refuge and strength and always ready to help in times of trouble.

How do you react when things go wrong? If you are a parent, do your children look up to you for reassurance that everything will be all right? If you are a leader, are your followers confident when they see your attitude? Take some time to identify and list the negative emotions that run through your body when things go wrong: jealousy, anger, greed, fear, hatred, revenge, and superstition. Which of these and others not listed can you identify? List them:

_____

_____

_____

No matter what you are going through, be patient and be determined that your problem will not see your end and that you will see the end of your problem. Your current trials have come to make you strong, even though you might not understand how they do. Be patient and stay positive. Be careful not to make a permanent decision over a temporary problem. Remember that ". . . those who trust in the Lord will find new strength. They will soar high on wings like eagles. They will run and not grow weary. They will walk and not faint."

2.3   Hear Positive, Speak Positive

"Just as the refiner's fire reveals the true character of precious metals, so the words we speak in times of crisis reveal our true character."

People are naturally good at saying sweet and thankful words as long as everything is going fine. But the moment adverse conditions arise and situations become unfavorable, praise escapes their lips and they blame everyone else—including God—for their problems. While you hope and trust for a change, you need to align your mouth with your heart when you are going through difficult times. Your mouth is the faucet that releases what is flowing in your heart. The pressure of life will one day turn that faucet on, and your true self will flow out, this is why it is important to think positive, look positive, be positive, and stay positive. If you do that, you will eventually speak positive.

What have you been telling yourself lately? What have you been telling others? Do you realize that your words are powerful? Do you know that your words can create your world? Do you realize that death and life are in the power of your tongue? Take some time to write down positive words of affirmation that you will repeat to yourself whenever life knocks you down. What you say is very powerful, so say something good, positive, and optimistic, and repeat it to yourself whenever you are tempted to say something negative.

_____

_____

_____

_____

_____

_____

There will always be hurdles to jump on your way to achieving your dreams. To leap over these hurdles and continue on your journey, you will need positive confessions, optimistic affirmations, and bold declarations. You must see mountains become plains and hills become lowlands. You must imagine visible things from invisible things. You must stay calm in the storm and see prosperity in adversity. You must see plenty in the midst of scarcity. Be careful how you respond when life challenges you; you just might get what you say.

2.4   Expect a Better Tomorrow

"Expectation is the mother of manifestation."

Everything, I mean everything, can change for your good within the next twenty-four hours, but you've got to believe it with unwavering faith in your heart and be courageous enough to declare it with your mouth. I repeatedly told myself that I was going to be an author and a speaker. It did not take long for what I spoke to happen.

When my diplomatic visa expired in 2006 and I became an illegal immigrant in the U.S.A., I declared that I was going to get my permanent residency and it happened just as I said four months later.

Take this time to write down what you want to see in the next twenty-four hours, next week, next month, next year, the next five years, and the next ten years. You have to be bold. If you doubt what you want to say, you had better not say it because you don't even believe it. But if you want to activate the power of words, write down the changes you want to see happen in your life and in your circumstances. Doing this takes boldness and a lot of faith:

_____

_____

_____

_____

_____

When you are done writing, do the following: Wherever you are right now, stand up if you can, walk around if you can, and boldly and loudly read aloud what you have just written down. What You Say Is What You Get. Your confession is your possession. Confess it for as many times as you wish until you feel it resonating in your heart, resounding in your soul, and vibrating in your body. You are loaded with possibilities; you cannot die—sitting on your potential.

When you refuse to blame others and take absolute responsibility for your failures, when you can stay calm when the storms of life are raging, when you can tune your ears to hear positive and your mouth to speak positive, when you expect a better tomorrow each day, every day, then you are in good posture for a miracle.

FAITH

"Be careful what you call impossible."

— *John Edmund Haggai*

*Before you begin: Please familiarize yourself with **Chapter 3** of Don't Die Sitting, pp. 43–47.*

It takes courage to speak prosperity in adversity. What if it did not happen? What if it took days, weeks, months, or years instead of twenty-four hours? Like the prophet, you, too, can make your dreams come through by speaking light into your dark situation, commanding calmness when life's storm is raging, calling the things that are not as though they are, talking strength when you feel weak, planning prosperity while still in adversity, preparing as a celebrity while still in obscurity, creating a vision board for the things you are hoping for, and a representation for the things you are yet to see.

3.1   See It Before You See It

*"You must be able to see the visible in **invisible**."*

Real faith is the bridge that can take you from the invisible to the impossible. You need the faith to see the invisible if you are going to do the impossible. You need to start showing the evidence of the things you want to see and physical proof of what you are still expecting. If you want to be an author, you must start writing and talking like an author before you become one. If you want to be a millionaire, you must start thinking and talking like a millionaire. If you want to be a pastor, start preaching without a pulpit. If you want to have your own business, start writing your business plan and networking with other business owners even if you are yet to register one. You have to be before you are; if you cannot be, it will not be. Start acting as if you are and you will soon be. It is better to act until you feel rather than waiting to feel before you act.

If you want to succeed in life and not die—sitting on your ideas, gifts, and potential—you need to take a trip to a nation called imagi-nation. You do not need a visa, and you will not pay any airfare to get to imagi-nation. There are no metal detectors, no pat-downs, and carry-on luggage is unnecessary. There is no class seating, no check-in time, and no connecting flight. All you have to do to get to this nation is to give yourself permission to go there.

Take some time right now to imagine where you want to be, what you want to see, where you want to live, how you want live, and/or whom you want to meet. You have to see it before you see it. What can you see?

_____

_____

_____

_____

_____

_____

_____

_____

_____

3.2   Can You See Anything?

"Faith can create something out of nothing."

Just as a symptom is an indication that a disease is present in the body, the steps you are taking by faith is a sign that something is about to happen. Faith is beyond the physical, and you might not understand it with your physical senses. A lot of people who claim to have faith really do not practice faith. Attending a religious service is not faith. If your vision is powerful enough to start working and walking right now with the intangibles of the things you are expecting, then you are a person of faith, but if you are waiting to see it so that you can believe it, you are simply religious. You have no faith.

If you don't want to die sitting, you will need the kind of faith that can see in your mind what you cannot see with your eyes. If you are not going to die with your song in you, you will need the kind of faith that can believe in the face of unbelief. Everything that you see in this world is déjà-vu. Someone has seen it (in their spirit) before you see it (in their senses). What can you see in your spirit? How can you begin to train your spiritual eyes to see what your physical eyes cannot see?

_____
_____
_____

When was the last time you traveled with your imagination? What can you see in your future right now? Remember, if you can't see it now, you won't see it then.

_____
_____
_____

3.3   Use the Power of Your Tongue

"Words are powerful; take them seriously. Your words can save you and your words can kill you."

What are you speaking with your mouth? Possibility or impossibility? Positivity or negativity? Prosperity or adversity? To create what you desire, your words and your actions need to be in sync with your thoughts, and what you say has to be consistent with what you see.

Write down some words of affirmation based on what you see with your spiritual eyes and read them aloud by faith in your personal, meditation, or prayer time. If you don't already have words of affirmation that you send to the atmosphere, create them!

_____
_____
_____
_____
_____

I hope you will begin to think positive and talk positive so that you can reach your desired destination. Be careful what you say with your mouth, and take your words seriously because they can happen just as you say them.

ABILITY IN DISABILITY

"He who excuses himself accuses himself."

— Anonymous

Before you begin: Please familiarize yourself with Chapter 4 of Don't Die Sitting, pp. 49–55.

During the difficult days in the city of Samaria, four ostracized and disadvantaged leprous men lived outside the city gate. Because of their contagious skin disease, they were declared unfit to stay in the city and unhealthy to live among the people. They were excluded from the commonwealth of Samaria and were homeless and jobless, separated from their family and friends. According to the social and religious laws of that time, they were not allowed to live with the so-called "normal" people. Though the lepers were physically challenged, they were mentally sound, which they proved when they later disowned their inadequacies and roused their conscious selves to action. They did something about their situation: they confronted their fear and put their faith to the test.

4.1   Don't Excuse Yourself

"It is self-defeating to think you cannot achieve greatness because of your background or past disappointments."

You won't achieve your dreams if you are always giving excuses, complaining about what you cannot do, and why you cannot do it. If what you are going through right now seems to be in direct contrast with your expectations, you have the perfect background to bring out the best in you. If you don't excuse yourself on the road to greatness, you will soon discover that the more you differ from your background, the greater your chance to succeed. Your background is the spring that will catapult you into your preferred future.

Excuses and complaints are clogs in the wheel of success. Vince Lombardi said

‚"Once you learn to quit, it becomes a habit." If you look long enough for a reason not to do what you are supposed to do, you will find an excuse. You promised that you would publish your book. Why have you not become a published author? You said you would exercise once a week. Why have you not been in the gym in the last two months? You set a goal to get out of debt. Why is your debt increasing instead of decreasing? You promised to go back to school this year. why have you not submitted an application?

Why have you not done what you promised yourself you were going to do? Voice your complaints and excuses in the space below. This is a conversation between you and yourself. I finally ground myself to create this workbook after confronting my excuses for not creating it a year after I published Don't Die Sitting. So, don't feel bad. Taking time to confront your excuses is a great way to identify them so that you can deal with them.

_____

_____

_____

_____

_____

_____

_____

_____

_____

Successful people are fully aware that a farmer who constantly watches the movements of the wind will never sow, and the one who waits for the cloud will never harvest. Don't sit there watching the wind. Stop complaining and do your work. Stop staring at the clouds, and get on with your life.

4.2   Don't Settle for Handicapped Parking

"Success is not a wish; it is work."

Have you ever wondered why healthy, normal people carry a disability badge in their car so that they can park in a handicapped parking spot? It's one of the things that still amaze me. Just as people who are not physically challenged carry the blue badge so that they can use handicap privileges, so do some people have a mental handicap badge hanging over their minds—incapacitated by the constant reminder that they are not fit to achieve greatness. Those who have achieved greatness in life did not necessarily have it easy; they worked through before their breakthrough. They were diligent when others were lazy; they were purposeful when others were aimless. Success is not a wish—it is work.

The limit is where you put it. What are the limiting beliefs you need to eliminate? You know you were supposed to have gone further in life than you have right now, but there is a handicap badge hanging on your subconscious mind preventing you from taking the limits off. Can you identify what is slowing you down? If you can identify your mental handicap badge, then you can get rid of it. Go ahead; write down your limiting beliefs.

_____

_____

_____

_____

_____

To achieve greatness, you need to release your limiting beliefs. You must pull out from the handicapped parking spot and let the world know that you are more than able. Leave that limiting label behind and start driving toward your future.

4.3 See the Ability in Disability

When you see anything that looks like a disability, remember that there is **ability** *inside di***sability**. *All you have to do is take "dis" out, whatever "dis" is for you.*

Your background, past disappointments, and lost opportunities are nothing compared to what is in store for your future. Don't disqualify yourself from winning in the race of life. If you look carefully both inward and forward, you will see that you, too, can win if you just try.

If you are limited today by your lack of a college education or because you are too tall, too short, too fat, too thin, too dark, too white, or even colorless, it is possible that you still have limiting beliefs. You have to start believing that your background and physical makeup were all designed to facilitate your success. Who you are is more important than what you are if only you can see that there is ability in your disability. Don't allow depression and low self-esteem to handicap you from getting to your Promised Land.

How do you rate your self-esteem? High? Average? Low?

_____

What do you see when you look at yourself in the mirror? A success? Just average? A failure?

_____

What are the things you don't like about your body? Too tall? Too short? Too dark? Too white? Albino? Big ears? Big nose? Abnormal head shape? Too fat? Too thin? Bad breath? Bad teeth arrangements? Etc. The list can go on. You have to be very honest with yourself and identify which of these are diminishing your self-esteem and eroding your confidence.

_____
_____
_____
_____
_____

Why are you not happy? Why are you gloomy, sensitive, and irritable? Think about it. Something is responsible for your low self-esteem and your depressive mood. The first step to winning the fight over your destiny is identifying what is stopping you and then determining to break through the obstacle:

_____
_____
_____

Whatever you are going through right now is nothing compared with what is going through you. Don't give up! If you are angry at yourself because of a missed opportunity, get over it and get ready to catch the next one. Don't live your life by other people's definition. You are wonderfully made, you are beautiful, you are handsome, and you are the best. When you see anything that looks like a disability, remember that there is ability inside disability. All you have to do is take "*dis*" out, whatever "*dis*" is for you.

HEROES AND "SHEROES"

"Look inside of you and be strong. . . A hero lies in you."

— *Mariah Carey*

*Before you begin: Please familiarize yourself with **Chapter 5** of Don't Die Sitting, pp. 57–68.*

During the heat of the 2008 presidential election in the United States, another remarkable event was taking place simultaneously in Beijing, China—the Twenty-Ninth Olympic Games.

5.1 Live an Impression

"Stop crying for what has left; be happy for what is left."

Are you living an impression or living with depression? Are you crying for what has left or happy for what is left? Write down what has left or who has left in this section, and then read them aloud and be thankful for them.

_____

_____

_____

_____

_____

_____

Despite their physical disadvantages, the heroes and sheroes in *Don't Die Sitting* wrestled their fears and conquered their inadequacies while the able-bodied spectators in the crowd cheered them on. You, too, can be happy now. Don't wait for any situation to make you happy, and don't count on someone to make you happy. Be happy now! Be thankful for what has left; be grateful for what is left.

5.2   Have Stars to Reach For

"I have always had a dream to take part in the Olympic Games, and losing my leg didn't change anything." — Natalie du Toit

Natalie du Toit's dream (*pp. 59–62*) of becoming an Olympic swimmer was shattered when she lost her left leg in a tragic motorcycle accident, but she decided to turn her stopping stone into a stepping stone. I'd like you to examine how Natalie was able to take advantage of her disadvantages:

At age six, Natalie dreamed of becoming an Olympic swimmer. At age seventeen, her dream was shattered when she lost her left leg in a tragic motorcycle accident. Do you have a childhood dream? What did you dream of becoming? Can you remember your childhood dream? I'd like you to write it down.

_____

_____

_____

What have you lost along the way that has dashed your hopes and shattered your childhood dreams? What have you lost that has caused you to stop believing that your dream can come true? Can you take some time to remember any dream-shattering event?

_____

_____

_____

The doctors could not save Natalie's left leg, so they were forced to amputate at the left knee. Now, I want you to pay attention to Natalie's attitude and her language a day after her leg was amputated: **She got out of bed the very next day** (*positive attitude*) and said, "I just wanted to get back to life again—swimming four hours a day—and I wanted to be able to walk again so that **I would be able to do things by myself** {*positive language*}." I had to emphasize these statements so that you can see how Natalie acted as if nothing had happened and how she was focusing on the ability in her disability.

I know that life's negative events have come between you and your dreams, but what is your attitude right now based on what you just read about Natalie? Will you wake up tomorrow and pursue your dreams, or will you continue to sleep in depression thinking about what you have lost? What will be your attitude toward your dreams, your goals, and your aspirations?

_____

_____

_____

Remember, if you allow what has left to stop you from using what is left, it means you believe that what has left is more powerful than what is left, and you are conceding that your nightmare is more powerful than your dreams. Although Natalie's physical body and circumstances changed drastically, her goals did not. What could have marked her end merely became her new beginning.

> *How badly do you want to fulfill your dreams? Which is stronger: your dreams or your nightmare? Natalie had every reason to hang the handicap badge on the mirror of her mind, but she refused. Don't allow your history to determine your destiny. Take the courage to write down your goals again with the mind and the attitude that you can and you will achieve them. Go ahead. Write down your dreams again:*

_____

_____

_____

_____

_____

Natalie defied all the odds that stood in her way. Less than two years after her accident, she qualified for the finals of the 800-meter freestyle at the 2002 Commonwealth Games and was named Outstanding Athlete. Although Natalie's physical body and circumstances changed drastically, her goals did not. What could have marked her end merely became a new beginning.

> *Can you picture yourself defying all the odds that are standing in your way right now? Think about how you can use these negative endings for a positive beginning. Life has handed you lemons, now is the time to take the lemons; get creative, and make some lemonade from them. Think of how you can use your bitterness for your betterment. Don't rush through this section because it is the turning point where you use your stumbling block as your stepping stone. Now think of all that has happened to you and how you can use this for what you want to happen.*

_____

_____

_____

_____

_____

_____

Natalie's motto is "Be everything you want to be." Before her accident, a coach gave her a poem. After the accident, Natalie rediscovered it. Originally, the poem had not meant much to her, but now a laminated copy hangs on her wall, and she can probably recite it in her sleep. The poem reads:

> *"The tragedy of life does not lie in not reaching your goals*
> *The tragedy of life lies in not having goals to reach for*
> *It is not a disgrace not to reach for the stars*
> *But it is a disgrace not to have stars to reach for."*

5.3   You Don't Need Eyes to Have a Vision

Stevie Wonder (*pp. 62–65*) is a Grammy Award–winning songwriter and a Rock and Roll Hall of Famer who did not allow his history to affect his destiny. Born blind as a premature baby, he had a serious automobile accident in his early twenties and suffered a permanent loss of his sense of smell. That was what happened, but Stevie Wonder took all that and succeeded as a singer and producer with album sales totaling more than 150 million units and was inducted into both the Rock and Roll Hall of Fame and the Songwriters Hall of Fame. Despite the accident, he recovered all his musical faculties, picked up his career and reappeared in concert a year later.

A year after his accident, Stevie Wonder recovered all of his musical faculties. What can you recover? To recover is to make up for a loss or damage to oneself. It is to regain the strength, composure, balance of oneself after being sick, wounded, or from an illness. You recover when you regain a former and better state or condition.

> *If you want to live a happy and a fulfilled life, you cannot afford to feel sorry about what you have lost. Rather, you need to recover, you need to make up for the loss, and you need to regain your strength, composure, and balance. You know you can do this. Write down the activities you used to do that make you feel alive and fulfilled. Identify the gifts and talents you have buried and*

rolled the stone against because life got in the way. Now is the time to recover all of them:

_____

_____

_____

_____

_____

_____

A year after his accident, Stevie Wonder picked up his career again. You too can pick up your book again, pick up your studies again, pick up your marriage again, pick up your career again, pick up your gifts and talents again, pick up your exercise again, and pick up yourself again. You must not die sitting!

It is not over until you win. You are not finished until you are done. You will not vanish until you finish. This is the time to pick it up again. Your life depends on it, your family is waiting on it, and your generation is waiting for it. What great project did you start doing that you have now abandoned? Write that down because it is time to pick it up again:

_____

_____

_____

_____

_____

_____

A year after his accident, Stevie Wonder reappeared in concert? Yes, he did. Like Natalie, Stevie did not allow what he lost to stop him from continuing to move ahead..

Where do you need to reappear? Who are you supposed to talk to? Write down places you need to go and people you need to meet to help you with your dream. If you have been there before and was discouraged, take courage because it is time to reappear. You can do this! The stage is all set, and it is time for you to appear again.

_____

_____

_____

_____

_____

_____

5.4   Stop Looking and Start Seeing

David Alexander Paterson is an American politician, the first black governor of New York City, and the first elected legally blind governor of any state. He is a blind governor who governs those who can see. While some blind people are street beggars and others are conditioned to pity, David Paterson defies the myth and sees with the vision locked behind his closed eyes.

What have you lost? What do you lack? Are you going to sit down depressed by what you can see or be inspired by what you cannot see? Remember, eyes that look are common, but eyes that see are rare. With all the tough situations you are looking at and thinking of right now, what can you see?

_____

_____

_____

Many people are walking the streets of life with their eyes wide shut, but blind visionaries such as Stevie Wonder and David Paterson did not allow their lack of sight to keep them from having a vision. Don't allow what you cannot see with your eyes to block the vision of what you can see with your heart.

5.5   Will You Complain?

The words "I can't" are not in Tawana's vocabulary. She trained herself to use her feet as hands. Tawana Williams was born without arms, but that did not stop her from being an author of three books, a poet, a vocalist, a wife, a mother, and the chief executive officer of Tawana Williams Outreach, Inc. In addition to singing, she can draw with her feet. If a woman who was born without arms has declared that she won't complain, I have also signed a declaration of independence from complaining about life's unpleasant situations. Worrying and complaining will not make things any better. You too might want you to sign this declaration of independence from complaints. You will find the *"Declaration of Independence from Complaining"* on the next page. Read it aloud to yourself and sign it.

The Declaration of Independence from Complaining

I,_____ hereby declare my independence from complaining about life and all of its unpleasant situations.

I will be thankful for all my problems
I will grateful for all my troubles
I will still be here when my troubles are gone

I will use the ability in disability
I will find hope in hopelessness
I will take the advantages in disadvantages
I will take courage in discouragement

I will stop crying for what has left
I will start rejoicing for what is left
I will stop worrying about who has left
I will start focusing on who is left

I will stop whining about what I don't have
I will start winning with what I have
I decide from today not to complain anymore about life
I will instead be grateful for everyone and everything
I will use my stumbling block as my stepping stone

So help me God.

_____   _____
          Sign   Date

One thing that amazed me about Tawana is that she trained herself to use her feet as hands. She decided not to whine about what she did not have but to win with what she had left.

Can you train yourself to win with what you have left, or will you spend the rest of life whining about what has left? Take some time to think of how you can win with what you have left:

_____

_____

_____

_____

_____

_____

Without arms, Tawana has written three books. I have two arms and have written only one book (at the time of writing this workbook). If Tawana can do it without arms, you can do it with two arms, one arm, or no arms.

No matter how disappointed you are with life or with people, don't complain! Instead, be thankful. The children of Israel did not get to their destination because they complained. Be thankful for who you are, where you are, what you have, and who you are with. Sing a song, laugh out loud, smile, rejoice, and be grateful, it could be worse, and it could have been you. Be thankful for life, be thankful for what you don't have, be thankful for all your losses. Be thankful! Be grateful! Be joyful! Don't worry. Be happy now!

Take some time to list some things you are thankful for:

_____

_____

_____

_____

_____

_____

_____

_____

_____

COUNT IT ALL JOY

"The greatest disability is that of the mind."

— Nick Vujicic

Before you begin: Please familiarize yourself with Chapter 6 of Don't Die Sitting, pp. 69–73.

Nicholas "Nick" Vujicic is an Australian evangelist, coach, and motivational speaker who has turned his problems to his opportunity. With over five million followers on Facebook and Twitter alone, Nick is very famous for his Life Without Limbs message but had his own share of lemons: born without arms or legs, hated his life, was depressed at age eight, attempted suicide at ten, hurt the very foot he used for typing, writing, and swimming at thirteen. "That injury made me realize that I need to be more thankful for my abilities and less focused on my disabilities," he said.

I have seen Nick speaking on stage, and he was so inspiring that you would not even think the brother is missing arms and legs; he is filled with an engaging sense of humor and living life to its fullest. His message is that it is fruitless to worry or complain about what you do not have. Nick has successfully processed all of life's lemons to make himself lemonade. What can you learn from this handsome but armless man?

6.1   Be Thankful

If you remember Tawana's story in Chapter 5 (*See 5.5., pp. 38*), she refused to complain about her disability but instead gave thanks for her ability. Nick adopted the same principle of giving thanks for what he has rather than what he lacked. I did a little exercise with my family during the 2013 Thanksgiving holiday—my wife and I and children took a clean sheet of paper and listed everything we were grateful for. Miranda was the most grateful, she listed 112 things she was grateful for; my 7-year-old, Deborah, and I had about 75 things we were thankful for; my 6-year-old, Ezra, listed about 70 things he was thankful for; and my-2-year-old, Jesse was thankful for one thing: mama's breast milk .

List at least 40 things you are thankful for. You will experience a feeling of gratitude before you finish this list.

_____   _____

_____   _____

_____   _____

_____   _____

_____   _____

_____   _____

_____   _____

_____   _____

_____   _____

_____   _____

_____   _____

_____   _____

_____   _____

_____   _____

_____   _____

_____   _____

_____   _____

_____   _____

_____   _____

_____   _____

Whenever you feel the urge to complain about what is going on in your life, let this list be a reminder that you have more than enough to be grateful for.

6.2   Concentrate On What You Have

Many people admire the cover of ***Don't Die Sitting***, but one thing that has struck me is when I hear people talk about the man on the book cover. He was running at dawn with an artificial limb on one leg and a running shoe on the other. I noticed that people are quick to talk about the artificial leg. Someone even called and asked if I am disabled and if I am the one on the book cover. Their comments reminded me that human beings are trained to naturally focus on the negative. However, I was surprised by my then 6-year-old Deborah's response when I asked her what she sees on the cover. She said, "The man has one bad leg but still has one good leg with which he could run." I was wowed by her response and I share her perspective whenever I talk about *Don't Die Sitting*.

I don't know you but here is what I know about you. You have what it takes if you will acknowledge it, develop it, use it, and deliver it. If you have been living for a while, I know you have lost some things, but no matter what you have lost in life up until now, I have no doubt that you still have something left. I read about a widow in Lebanon who received a miracle with a handful of flour and a little olive oil. I've heard about how a little boy's fish sandwich was used to feed five thousand people in the desert. The four lepers in this book used the strength they had left to end a deadly siege and feed a whole city.

You have been thankful for all the things you have lost in life. Now take some time to write down the things you have left. Write as many things as you can remember because the things you write here represent the raw materials for your miracle, the seed for your harvest, and the cloud that will pour for you an abundance of rain.

_____

_____

_____

_____

_____

_____

_____

_____

6.3   Dream Big

Nick loves swimming, but growing up, he feared he was going to swim through life alone. He had doubts that he would ever get married or meet anybody who would love him or spend the rest of her life with him. Four years before meeting his wife, Nick started dreaming of finding a wife and becoming a parent. Four years later, he is married to his beautiful wife, Kanae, and they are both blessed with a baby boy named Kiyoshi. Nick continues to encourage everyone that "happiness does not come from temporary things, because if you want happiness and go to temporary things, your happiness will be temporary." Nick definitely did not allow what he did not have to stop him from dreaming big and hoping for a brighter future. Talking about his wife, "Dreams do come true."

Write three to five things you dream of having but think you can never achieve because of what you are currently experiencing. Remember to dream big—dreams do come through.

_____

_____

_____

_____

_____

_____

Let the story of Nick Vujicic encourage you, and refuse that depression will influence your life in any way. Set your mind firmly on the goal you would like to accomplish, because vision has a way of inspiring you to keep moving forward, and dreams do come through.

6.4   Turn Your Wheelchair into Your "Wheelcheer"

Not many people knew Yinka when he was a freelance broadcasting journalist; however, this Nigerian-born music entertainer and recording artist became famous after his spinal cord was damaged in an automobile accident. Despite his setback, Yinka has worked hard to turn his life around by using his musical and vocal talents (what he has left). Yinka still has his wheelchair, but he has turned it into his "wheelcheer"—making music, touring the world, and entertaining with his *"tungba"* music.

I'd like you to think a little more on what seems like a problem, a challenge, or a backlash to you right now. What creative things can you begin to do with this unfortunate situation?

_____

_____

_____

6.5   Shame on Us

George Washington said, "Ninety-nine percent of all failure comes from people who make excuses." Are you part of that 99 percent, or are you part of the 1 percent who will do whatever it takes to realize their dreams? If you excuse yourself, you will only accuse yourself.

I have borrowed the following thought from Stevie Wonder's song *"So What the Fuss?"* from his 2005 album *A Time to Love* and rendered my own version:

If I have two arms and legs and am depressed while those without legs or arms are motivated and motivating others, shame on me.

If you complain about what you don't have when you can maximize and profit from what you do have, shame on you.

If we blame our origination for not reaching our destination, shame on us!

PART TWO

Chances

What are the odds?

QUESTIONS

"Learn from yesterday, live for today, hope for tomorrow. The most important thing is not to stop questioning."

— Albert Einstein

*Before you begin: Please familiarize yourself with **Chapter 7** of Don't Die Sitting, pp. 77–86.*

Great people are almost always associated with great thinking. Great thinkers were not necessarily born great, but they become great by giving themselves the permission to dream, fantasize, doodle, meditate, and think outside the box. They ask questions, challenge the status quo, and always want to improve on what they have already made better.

7.1   Ask Questions

"You only get answers to the questions you ask." — *John C. Maxwell*

If you desire deliverance from debt, an abusive relationship, poverty, a reckless lifestyle, stagnation, or any other undesirable circumstance, you must start asking yourself questions about your life. If you have reached this point in this workbook, I congratulate you. I have no doubt that you are serious about maximizing your potential because you took the time to thoughtfully and truthfully answer the questions that are being asked in this workbook. It is only those who ask that receive.

In section 1.1., you listed your BIGGEST challenges. In 2.2, you promised not to blame anyone or anything for your problems.

Now, I want you to ask yourself, "Why am I not progressing as I should?" "Why am I not maximizing my potential?" I would encourage you to provide an honest answer to the "why?" questions. Remember, everything changed for the four lepers when they ask, "Why are we just sitting here waiting to die?" They did not ask, "Why did they drive us out of the city?" or "Why did the law not favor us?" They took responsibility and asked themselves questions. You, too, should ask yourself: "Why am I not getting the results I wanted? "What am I doing here?" "Why is this happening to me?" "Where did I go wrong?" or "Why am I broke?" "Why am I stuck?" What other questions can you ask yourself about your current situation?

_____

_____

_____

_____

_____

_____

7.2   Think—Don't Stink

While the normal and healthy people in Samaria confined themselves to the city, stinking in their mess, the four diseased lepers were thinking about a way out of their mess. I once read that losers focus on what they are going through, while winners focus on where they are going to. The four lepers knew death was inevitable if they remained where they were, so they started thinking about where they wanted to go. They asked themselves, "Why not move forward?" While the people in the city were "stinking," the lepers were thinking.

Is it possible that you are getting the wrong answers in life because you are not asking the right questions? Here are some questions you could ask yourself to get you started on the path of critical thinking: Why? Why not? Why me? Why not me? Why now? Why not now? If not now, when? If not me, who? You can think your way out of your current messy situation if you can take time to ask yourself some critical questions.

Think again about the BIGGEST challenges you have right now (review your thoughts in section 1.1) Ask yourself, "Why? Why not? Why me? Why not me? Why now? Why not now? If not now, when? If not me, who?" Your response to these critical questions might help you to discover the opportunities in your problems .

_____

_____

_____

_____

_____

_____

_____

_____

_____

7.3   Question the Answers You Are Getting

Newton's first law of motion states that an object will remain at rest or in uniform motion unless acted upon by an external force. The same law is applicable when it comes to turning your life around. You will continue to experience what you are experiencing or remain where you are unless you take action. You will continue to get the answers you are getting until you ask a different question. It is not enough to answer life's questions; you must also question life's answers. You will continue to get the same answers until you question them.

If you are broke, it is an answer to the questions you have asked up to now. To get a different answer, you need to question the current answer. The lepers asked, "Why should we sit here waiting to die?" The lost (prodigal) son asked, "How many of my father's hired men have more than enough bread, but I am dying here from hunger?" God asked Ezekiel, "Son of man, can these bones become living people again?" Before killing Goliath, David asked, "What will be done for the man who kills this Philistine and removes this disgrace from Israel?"

> *Life has given you some answers. If you are not going to die sitting, you need to start questioning those answers. Remember, you will continue to get the answers you are getting unless you ask a different question. Now, go ahead and question the answers life has given you or is giving you right now:*

_____

_____

_____

_____

_____

_____

Ask questions, and think critically. You just might be the answer you are looking for.

7.4   Know That the Reality of Life Is Death

"The fear of death might stop you, but it cannot, and will not, stop death."

Death is inevitable; we will all die. I will die. You will die. It does not matter to me anymore if death comes by a plane crash, a motor accident, from chronic disease, or from a gunshot. Whatever the cause, I have learned that the reality of life is death. If you want to go anywhere in life, you must accept the fact that death is inevitable. The fear of death might stop you, but it cannot, and will not, stop death.

It is widely believed that your behavior and action are controlled by your beliefs and philosophy. What you hold as true concerning death may be affecting the way you approach life. What are your beliefs about death and longevity?

_____

_____

_____

_____

_____

_____

It is possible that you are postponing or procrastinating on what you ought to do right now because of your philosophy about life and death. You will most likely put off till next month what you are supposed to do this month if you think you are going to be here next month. But what will you do differently if you know that you will not be here next month?

Let us assume you have three months to live (we all plan and pray to live long, this is just an assumption), what goals would you like to accomplish? What would you want to do for your parents? How will you want to be remembered?

_____

_____

_____

7.5   Take Your Chances

Great risks always come with great rewards. There is no gain without pain. There is no testimony without a test.

In the midst of the famine that struck their city, the lepers determined not to die—sitting on the same spot. Though a tough situation was at hand, they took time to consider the choices before them. Each opportunity held a different degree of risk, and only one offered even a slim opportunity for survival:

First choice: <u>Go back to the city</u>: The city of Samaria represented their past. The lepers contemplated going back to their past, although they knew there was no food in the city and the people there were trapped and starving.

Second Choice: <u>Stay put at the city gate</u>: The lepers ruled out going back to their past and moved on to debate their present. They considered staying put at their current location—outside the city gate and remain idle there until they die.

Third Choice: <u>Go on to the camp of their enemy</u>: After they decided to neither go back to their past nor sit until they there in their present position, the four lepers engaged in conversation about their future—the military camp of their enemy. This was the only place where they might have a chance to live, but it was also a place where they might be killed, depending on the judgment of their enemy.

You have listed the BIGGEST challenges you are facing right now in section 1.1. You took time to critically think about how you got into this messy situation in section 7.2. If you remember the story of Yinka Ayefele in section 6.4., you wrote down some creative things you will begin to do to turn your situation around. You can revisit and revise them before answering this next question.

No matter how tough or how tight your situations are, you have options, and there is a way out. You just haven't found it yet. For the toughest situation you are facing right now, can you think of up to ten different things you could do right now to help turn the situation around?

_____

_____

_____

_____

_____

_____

_____

Of the ten things you listed, identify the top three that are toughest to implement:

_____

_____

_____

Of the ten things you listed, identify the top two that might give you the highest return and greatest reward:

_____

_____

_____

Great risks come with great rewards. If the top two options that will give you the greatest reward are the same as the two options that are the toughest to implement, you might want to follow-through on these options. But if they are different, consider implementing the four options.

DEFINING MOMENTS

"Your time is not the time to take your time."

— *Saji Ijiyemi*

*Before you begin: Please familiarize yourself with **Chapter 8** of Don't Die Sitting, pp. 87–94.*

The four lepers had become irrelevant in their city. The government would never have selected them to spy out the camp of the invaders, but with the current unfavorable situation in their city coupled with the lepers' determination not to die sitting, they sensed a defining moment, and time picked them.

8.1   Don't Go Back

Your defining moment is not the time to retreat or regret. It is the time to seize the moment. You can never replay yesterday. If you are still keeping the memory of past hurts and disappointments alive, you are probably still plugged into the past. As Joe Vitale puts it in his book *The Attraction Factor,* "A part of your energy is still back there, reliving and probably re-creating the old event." If you want to live a legacy, you have to let go of your regrets, past hurts, disappointments, and also forgive those that might have hurt you in the past.

If there are unresolved events that still hurt you silently, you have to let it go. If there are people in your past that still negatively run your life in the present, you have to forgive them, release them, and let them go. Take some time to write down some things in the past that still hurt you, find a place to read them aloud to yourself, release them, and let them go. You will be glad you did:

_____

_____

_____

_____

_____

_____

8.2   Don't Stay Here

Stagnant water stinks.

Holding onto your past can hinder you from moving into your future. Maintaining the status quo in the present can also keep you from moving forward. The lepers knew that their future was quite uncertain, but they also knew that the present is not guaranteed either. This is why they decided to move boldly into their future. If you are not growing, you are dying; if you are not living, you are dying. It is time for you to move to your next level. Now is the time to take your chance.

8.3   Take Your Chance

"Let's take our chances. . . we've got nothing to lose."

The lepers knew their future was filled with unforeseen dangers, but they went anyway. "We have got nothing to lose," they said. You also have nothing to lose if you can seize the moment and start working to make your dreams come true. If you fail, you will not be the only person who has ever failed; if you succeed, again you will not be the only one. Don't wait to pick a time to make your dreams happen. Time has picked you. this is your finest hour—it's time to launch!

If you want to write a book, start a business, or pioneer a TV show, this is not the time to take your time. This is the time to take your chance. You have nothing to lose. It is true that tomorrow is not certain, but it is not promised either. Write down those BIG ideas you would like to take a chance on:

_____

_____

_____

8.4   You Can't Get There If You Stay Here

"You cannot get there if you stay here."

It is good to have a vision of where you want to go in life, but it is even better to start moving in that direction. By faith, Father Abraham left his native country although he was not clear on where he was going. By faith he lived as a foreigner in a country he would later receive as his own. He did not receive the country first and then decide to go there. He went to the country first and later received it as an inheritance.

Like Abraham, the four lepers went to the camp of the Syrian army, not knowing whether they would live or die. Abraham received his promise because he moved, and the lepers ultimately survived because they moved. You, too, can achieve your dream if you will overcome your fear and start moving in the direction of your destination. Your dream is achievable, but it might not come on a platter. It's time to move in the direction of your future. You've been on your mark, and you've been getting set. Now is the time to go! You cannot get there if you stay here.

Those who have left their footprints in the sand of history are people who are on the move. They are not complacent. They are not sedentary. They love adventure, and they are curious. It is time to stop talking about what you are going to do and start doing what you are talking about. Write down the immediate actionable steps you will start taking today to achieve your goals:

Success is progress. Keep moving if you want to get there.

PART THREE

Choices

We make them, and then they make us

GO!

"Playing safe is probably the most unsafe thing in the world. You cannot stand still. You must go forward."

— Robert Collier

Before you begin: Please familiarize yourself with **Chapter 9** *of Don't Die Sitting, pp. 97–104.*

9.1   The Choice is Yours

Although you cannot change your past, you can decide what you want in your future by the choices you make in the present. I made a choice fourteen years ago, and my choice made me fourteen years later. If you do not want to die sitting on your potential, you have to make some difficult choices. Your present life is the sum total of all the decisions you have made up to this point, and you can peek into what your life will look like ten years from now by the decisions you make today.

The decisions you make today will make you tomorrow. Review your response to Section 8.3. You will have to make some tough choices if you want to achieve your goals. You might have to make some tough choices concerning your family, your friends, your environment, who you spend your time with, what you spend your money on, who you listen to, what you listen to, the programs you watch on TV, how much time you spend on Facebook, Twitter, and other social media, etc. The list can go on but you know the decisions you have to make if you want to live a meaningful life. What tough decisions are you willing to make if you want to accomplish your goals?

_____

_____

_____

_____

_____

_____

The choice, as they say, is yours.

9.2   Small, Medium, Large, or Mega?

"You cannot choose where you came from, but you can decide where you want to end up."

On page 100–102 of **Don't Die Sitting**, I told the story of my first trip to the United States. The story taught me that life is truly full of options, and we confuse ourselves and others if we don't know what to choose.

While the choice of what to eat or drink is trivial, some choices in life are crucial. How big is your dream? Small, medium, large, or mega? The choice is yours. You will decide the size of your dreams, the size of your goals, and the size of your influence. Life will not force it on you. If you dream small, do not envy those who dream big; if you dream big, do not be jealous of those who have mega dreams. Life has a way of giving each of us what we want. The choice, again, is yours.

Review your response to section 5.2. You will recall that Natalie du Toit dreamed of becoming an Olympic swimmer and she started early, at the age of six. How BIG is your dream? Circle one below:

Small   Medium   Large   Mega

If you think your dream is not big enough, I encourage you to have a megasized dream. Remember that it is always impossible until it is done.

9.3   Two-Thirds of the Name of God Is Go!

"Be on the way, not in the way."

After much deliberation, the four lepers bade farewell to their past, said good-bye to their present, and started marching toward their future. They spent the day deliberating their options, but when evening came, they made the decision and got up and went there. If you want to get to your destination, it is time to put some wheels to your faith and start moving to your next level. Like the four lepers, determine to survive, and then get up and march on by faith.

Planning, brainstorming, deliberating, strategizing, researching, etc., are all useless professional exercise if you are not going to get up and go take action. The purpose for writing *Don't Die Sitting* is to inspire and motivate you to get out of your comfort zone so that you can get to your glory zone. If you are not going to stand up and go make your life happen, then you have decided to be in the way, not on the way.

In section 1.2, you wrote down the steps you are going to take tomorrow, next week, or next month to address your challenges. Please review what you wrote down in section 1.2, and decide right now that you will simply go and take those steps. Come back sometime later to document your experience in the space below. Please do not write anything in this space until you have taken action on what you promised to do.

_____

_____

_____

_____

_____

_____

_____

_____

In section 5.2, you wrote down some of your childhood dreams, goals, and aspirations. Please review what you wrote down in Chapter 5.2, and decide right now that you will simply go and start working on your dreams, goals, and aspirations. Come back sometime later to document your experience in the space below. Please do not write anything in this space until you have taken action on what you promised to do.

_____

_____

_____

_____

_____

Also in section 5.2, you wrote down specific actions you intend to take to turn your negative endings into positive beginnings, your lemons into lemonade, and your bitterness into betterment. Please review what you wrote down in Chapter 5.2, and decide right now that you will simply go and take action to turn life's lemons into lemonade. Come back sometime later to document your experience in this space. Please do not write anything in the space below until you have taken action on what you promised to do.

In Chapter 5.3., Stevie Wonder recovered all his musical faculties after his accident. You, too, have identified some things you need to recover or recover from. Please review what you wrote down in Chapter 5.3, and decide right now that you will simply go and take action on the things you need to recover or recover from. Come back sometime later to document your experience in the space below. Please do not write anything in this space until you have taken action on what you promised to do.

Also in Chapter 5.3., Stevie Wonder picked up his career again after his accident. You, too, should pick up again some abandoned projects, ideas, gifts, and talents. Please review what you wrote down in Chapter 5.3, and decide right now that you will simply go and take action on things you promised to pick back up. Come back sometime later to document your experience in the space below. Please do not write anything in this space until you have taken action on what you promised to do.

GODLY CHOICES

"The choice is yours: make it good, and make it Godly."

— *Saji Ijiyemi*

*Before you begin: Please familiarize yourself with **Chapter 10** of Don't Die Sitting, pp. 105–117.*

The Bible is full of men and women who made great and godly decisions. The lost son eventually chose a better life at home with his father. Joseph rejected an offer of sex from his boss's wife. The three Hebrew boys resolved not to bow down and worship a golden image. Esther dared to go before the king unannounced. Daniel refused to defile himself with the king's food or wine. Nehemiah left his position in the palace to rebuild his home country's broken walls. Job decided not to curse God after he lost everything and became sick to the point of death.

10.1   Where You Are Is Not Who You Are

"If you don't like where you are, change it. You're not a tree."

— *Jim Rohn*

The story of the lost son, popularly called the prodigal son, will inspire you, especially if you feel hopeless, helpless, and stuck in life. In his disappointed and desperate state, the lost son came to his senses, had a conversation with himself, crafted a plan, made a choice, and followed through with action. His deliverance started the moment he began to talk to himself—asking himself questions on how he ended up homeless, hungry, and helpless. He got tired of the way he was living and remembered that even the servants in his father's house had enough to eat.

If you are not very satisfied with where you are or who you have become, it is time to return to your real self and seize this opportunity to make a better choice. Like the lost son, it might be time for you look in the mirror and have a real talk with yourself

If you do not like the way you are living right now, it might be because you have left the place where you are celebrated for the place where you are tolerated. If you are not excited about the life you are living, you have to change it if you do not want to die sitting. This is the time to have a conversation with yourself. Reflect on where you are in life right now and ask yourself: "Am I better than my current environment?" Write down your thoughts:

_____

_____

_____

10.2   Act—Don't React!

"Maybe you were made . . . for such a time as this."

Esther was at a crossroads. There was a conspiracy to wipe out her race and she, being the queen, was in the best position to save her people. She was faced with difficult choices: she could keep silent, betting on the fact that she was the queen and no one would kill her; she could also go before the king without invitation and lose her own life in an attempt to save others. Like the four lepers who chose the danger of the future over the comfort of the present, Esther chose to appear before the king uninvited, a move that carried a death penalty unless the king held out his golden scepter to welcome her. Esther's brave decision paid off. She appeared before the king without an invitation. The king held out the golden scepter to spare her life, and she saved her entire race from destruction.

What would have happened to the Jews in the 127 provinces of Mede and Persia if Esther had kept silent for fear of her own life? What if she had refused to go before the king? Like her uncle, Mordecai, told her, "Don't think that just because you live in the king's house you're the one Jew who will get out of this alive. If you persist in staying silent at a time like this, help and deliverance will arrive for the Jews from someplace else, but you and your family will be wiped out."

In section 7.4, you learned that death is inevitable. No matter how long you plan to live, you will die one day. The question is: "Are you going to die reacting to life or die acting on life? I would like you to take some time to think about the influence, the opportunities, and the connections you have right now. Is it possible that you have been placed in your current position for such a time as this? Is it possible that you have favor with the government and people of influence to make life better for some people? Think about it and write down the names of people who might benefit from your influence:

_____

_____

_____

_____

_____

_____

You might be the solution to the troubles in your family, your community, your race, or your country. Will you keep silent when everyone is depending on you to speak? Will you risk your life to save your family or your country? This is your time to accept some measure of risk. This is your time to act, because it might be too late if you wait to react.

10.3   Don't Bow Under Pressure

What will you not do even if there is nobody watching?

Hananiah, Mishael, and Azariah were three prisoners of war carried away from Jerusalem to Babylon. They were strong, healthy, good-looking young men who learned the language and literature of a foreign land. They were well educated and well positioned to serve in the royal palace. When the command of their earthly king in Babylon contradicted the command of their heavenly King, the Hebrew boys chose to obey the King of kings and they got a fiery punishment for disobeying the king in Babylon.

If you are going to live a life of impact, you must have some core values and personal code of ethics you are not going to break no matter the consequences. Your core values are your fundamental beliefs that dictate your actions and behaviors and guide your choices and decisions. The three Hebrew boys did not stammer in letting the king know that they would not bow to another god besides Yahweh. They had settled on what they would (and would not) do before the situation ever arose. When their earthly king's command was opposite to that of their heavenly King, they did not try to deliberate or negotiate what to do. They simply responded and decided based on their fundamental beliefs and core values.

If you want to live a life that will impact others, you need to be a person of integrity and settle on your core values. What will you not do even if there is nobody watching? What will you not compromise on when it comes to your spouse, your children or your loved ones? What will you not do when dealing in business? What governs what you do? What do you stand for? Take some time to write down your top five core values:

_____

_____

_____

_____

_____

_____

Take these values with you everywhere you go and let them be the yardstick for everything you say and do.

10.4   Don't Do Wicked Things

How could I do such a wicked thing?

Joseph was sold into slavery as a teenager. He was serving dutifully in the house of his master when his boss's wife offered him free sex. Joseph told her that would be a wicked thing to do and a detestable sin against God. Before Mrs. Potiphar could go any further with her sexual advances, Joseph fled the scene. As expected, the woman was enraged by Joseph's refusal and falsely accused him of rape. Joseph lost favor with his master and ended up in prison—the same prison where the king's prisoners were held. Joseph quickly realized that Mrs. Potiphar was nothing more than a wrong exit on the highway to his destiny and he refused to do what he considered a wicked thing.

> *Like Joseph, you will count anything that wants you to compromise your core values as wicked. Based on your core values in section 10.3, what behaviors would you consider wicked? What are the things you would walk or run away from no matter how pleasurable they seem?*

_____

_____

_____

_____

_____

10.5   Keep at It!

"Shortcuts to prosperity can cut you short."

As Joseph moved from Potiphar's house to the Pharaoh's prison, he was drawing closer to his destiny, though he might not have realized it. He was on his way to his purpose although through a painful process. One important thing to note as Joseph moved from his people to Potiphar's house and to the prison, is that he continuously used his gift (interpreting dreams), and he never diminished his excellent work ethic (home cleaning and janitorial services). Although his position was changing, his performance never changed—he kept performing with excellence until his gift and his work ethic took him to the palace. He arrived in Egypt as a slave, but he kept at it until he rose to become the prime minister in his land of slavery.

If you do not want to die sitting, you have to keep doing excellent work no matter how unfavorable the situation. You cannot quit, you cannot give up, and you cannot give in. In the end, you will win, but you must be willing to go through until you get through. No matter how bad things are in society or how worse the situation seems, it is your opportunity to hone your natural gifts and talents, master your craft, and improve your work ethic. Joseph did not know that the prison was the last stop before the palace. Never, never give up! Keep at it! You are closer than you think.

When everything was working against Joseph, he had two things working for him: his natural gift of interpreting dreams and his excellent work ethic in home cleaning and janitorial services. You will also need these two companions when you are in the valley of life.

_____

_____

_____

What are your natural gifts and talents? These will make room for you and bring you before kings:

_____

_____

_____

On a scale of 1–10, how would you rate your work ethic under unfavorable situations? Circle one:

1   2   3   4   5   6   7   8   9   10

There are tollgates on the way to your destination. You might have to go back to school, take online courses, exercise regularly, stick to a diet, or cut back on sleep. You might have to pray more, fast more, forgive more, or draw closer to God. You might have to save more and spend less. You might have to love the unlovable and be willing to do the ridiculous before you can attain the miraculous. Your present life is a result of your past choices. If you are not pleased with how your life is turning out, it is time to start making godly choices.

PART FOUR

Changes

It must start with you

MIRACLES ALONG THE WAY

"You are either on the way or in the way."

— Author Unkown

*Before you begin: Please familiarize yourself with **Chapter 11** of Don't Die Sitting, pp. 121–129.*

The four lepers acknowledged their inadequacies, considered their chances, chose from available options, and were ready to march down the road to their change. They had no idea they would become heroes when they left their comfort zone to venture into the danger zone. It was not their strength that prompted them to rise up and act; rather, it was their desire and determination not to die—sitting on their potential.

11.1   Arise!

". . . after the sun went down they got up"

The four lepers left the complacency of the present to explore the possibilities of the future. If you can rise up when everything is going down, you will have the victory. I cannot say what might happen as you summon the courage to confront your desired future, but I can say that the miracle you are expecting might not be located where you are right now; you might just find it along the way.

By now, I believe you are inspired to bet on yourself (section 8.3), and you are determined to get out of your comfort zone to explore what the future has for you (section 9.3). As you decide to make your life count, be prepared because obstacles will come your way, and you will sometimes be discouraged. But if you can promise yourself to look up when everything is looking down and rise up when everything else has fallen down, you will see miracles along the way.

Use the space below to promise yourself that: you will find courage when *dis**courage**ment comes, you will hold onto the hope in **hope**lessness, you will take the advantage in dis**advantage**, and you will always remember that there is ability in dis**ability**. Promise?*

_____

_____

_____

The lepers did not experience a divine stirring until they started moving. You too have to get moving. You, too, have to get moving. You have to get going if you want to experience the miracles along the way.

11.2   The Lord Factor

"The Lord Factor is simply God stepping into your situation and acting on your behalf, sometimes even without your knowledge of the process."

I believe you have read the story on how God saved me from being run over by a train (pp. 124–126 of **Don't Die Sitting**). Up to now, I cannot explain how I survived death; all I know is that I am alive today because of The Lord Factor, which is simply God stepping into your situation and acting on your behalf, sometimes even without your knowledge of the process.

While they were on their way, God amplified the steps of these weakened and weary lepers and made them sound like the marching of a great army. The divine amplifier scared their enemies, and as a result, their threats panicked and fled.

Have you ever survived a situation that seemed impossible? Have you ever survived a major life crisis? Have you ever survived an accident and have no clue how? That is The Lord Factor at work. Think about three major instances in your life where you survived an "impossible" situation and cannot even explain how:

_____

_____

_____

_____

_____

_____

_____

_____

_____

The next time you feel trapped in a seemingly impossible situation, let the testimonies above serve as a reminder that the God that saw you through those will surely see you through this.

11.3 All Fear Is Gone

"Because He lives, I can face tomorrow."

— Bill and Gloria Gaither

The four lepers did not have a clue as to what was waiting for them in the camp of their enemy, but they were determined to go there anyway. After traveling all night, they finally reached the edge of the Syrian army's encampment, but to their amazement, they found no one was there—only food, drink, clothes, silver, gold, and everything else the lepers needed.

I believe there is greatness in you and there is greatness in your future, but you are allowing fear to lock you out of it. I want to reassure you that you have what it takes to confidently face the future and explore the greatness that is inside you. Your life and your future are worth exploring just because God lives.

I would like you to answer this question and always remember it whenever you think of quitting: "Will you allow the risks of pursuing your dream to outweigh the rewards of accomplishing your dreams?

☐   Yes   ☐   No

If you answer "No," fear is still immobilizing you, and you will not move. If you answer "Yes," keep on moving—the future is brighter than you think.

12

GIVE BACK

"Non sibi sed aliis." (Not for ourselves but for others)

— Latin Proverb

*Before you begin: Please familiarize yourself with **Chapter 12** of Don't Die Sitting, pp. 131–136.*

The Samaritan lepers have now arrived at the military base of the enemy army, but to be sure that the Syrian army was not trying to ambush them, the lepers first surveyed the entire base. After they were certain their fear was truly groundless, they went from one tent to another, eating, drinking, and stockpiling gold, silver, and clothing for themselves until one of them realized they were not doing the right thing.

12.1   Do What Is Right: Share

"This is not right. This is a day of good news, and we are not sharing it with anyone!"

The lepers were not under any obligation to share their newfound wealth with anyone; after all, they had paid the price to get where they were. Reflecting on their attitude toward prosperity, the lepers realized that all the wealth now at their disposal should not be for themselves alone but also for others. A lot of wealthy and influential people today hardly help anyone with their abundance. They never think for a moment that God might have brought them to a place of abundance so that He could use them as an instrument to bless others.

With hard work and God's help, I am sure you will surely succeed in your life's pursuit. But do you have a plan to give back and share your success with others? If you do not already have a "Giving Plan," you might want to start preparing one. Consider which cause you will support—financially. Which group

71

or nonprofit organization (NGO) you will donate to? Who in your family, society, or country could benefit from your wealth? What community project are you going to fund? Whose child can you sponsor? It does not have to be something big or complex. Just list who or what you will give to and support if you have the resources:

_____

_____

_____

_____

_____

_____

_____

_____

12.2   Don't Repay Evil for Evil

Never repay evil with evil

After the lepers realized they were not doing the right thing by keeping quiet about information that could benefit their fellow citizens, they decided to go back home and share the good news with the king and the people that expelled them from the city because of their disability. Despite how they had been treated by their own people, the lepers still decided to share their newfound wealth with their fellow citizens. Joseph did the same thing when he showed compassion and took care of his brothers though he had the opportunity and the position to pay them back for all the wrong they had done to him. But he decided not to pay back their evil with evil. Joseph said he was not God that he should punish his brothers; he realized that the opportunity to be prime minister in Egypt was not intended as a blessing for him alone, but was intended by God to save many people.

If you are blessed, celebrated, and wealthy, a leader, or a celebrity, do you agree that all you have and all you are is not for you alone, but for others also?

☐   Yes   ☐   No

Have you considered that you are in such a lofty position so that you can help many people?

☐   Yes   ☐   No

BELIEVE

"What you say is what you get."

— Saji Ijiyemi

*Before you begin: Please familiarize yourself with **Chapter 13** of Don't Die Sitting, pp. 137–142.*

Miracles do happen, even if you don't believe in them Miracles happen when the divine chooses to work through human instruments. However, because of our limited physical senses, we tend not to believe in miracles. If you are facing an impossible situation and it seems there is no way out, you can still experience a miracle if you will believe and have faith that what is impossible with man is possible with God.

13.1   Believe So You Can See

"What you believe is what you become."

The human race is divided on who created the earth and the seven billion people living on it. Theories abound as to how life on earth began. While discoveries and advancements in science, technology, and engineering have greatly helped us understand the world we live in, they cannot explain most divinely orchestrated miracles.

While science seeks explanation for anything and everything, the working of miracles is by faith. Every human attempt to explain the divine will always result in frustration and eventually in unbelief.

To believe is "to have confidence in the truth, the existence, or the reliability of something, although without absolute proof that one is right in doing so" (dictionary.com). So, if you want to see in your life what you see in your spirit, you have to have confidence that what you expect will happen even when there is no proof that it will. Write down the top five things you believe concerning

73

your goals, dreams, and future:

1. I believe that..._____

_____

_____

2. I believe that..._____

_____

_____

3. I believe that..._____

_____

_____

4. I believe that..._____

_____

_____

5. I believe that..._____

_____

_____

13.2 Believe in Miracles

What if some do not believe?

The king in Samaria questioned the lepers' report of abundance. He could not believe that his city could go from scarcity to abundance in just twenty-four hours. Instead of believing that God could miraculously provide food, drink, clothes, silver, and gold for his starving citizens, the king merely sat in his palace, analyzing the miracle and thinking the news must be false. His city had been delivered from the siege of the enemy, but he could not believe it.

I assume you must have heard the popular saying that "if it seems too good to be true, it probably is." Although this statement is very good, some people have built a limited belief system on the foundation of that statement. If you want the magic of believing to work in your life, you should not allow clichés such as this to limit your belief system. Answer the following questions sincerely:

1. Does it seem too good to be true that you can be debt free? ☐ Yes   ☐ No

2. Does it seem too good to be true that you can go back to school? ☐ Yes ☐ No

3. Does it seem too good to be true that you can start all over again? ☐ Yes ☐ No

4. Does it seem too good to be true that you can find a solution to the problem facing your community? ☐ Yes ☐ No

5. Does it seem too good to be true that you, yes, you, can be a speaker, inspiring millions with your voice? ☐ Yes ☐ No

6. Does it seem too good to be true that you can run for a political office in your country and win? ☐ Yes ☐ No

Since you are the only one who knows you best, I'd like you to think about some areas of your life where you are expecting a miracle but have allowed your limiting beliefs to minimize your expectation. You want to reaffirm in the space below that some miraculous things can still happen to you by favor with little to no labor from you. You know what it is, so go ahead and reaffirm them. Believe! Believe!! Believe!!! Complete these statements:

_____

_____

_____

_____

_____

_____

_____

_____

_____

What if some did not believe? Don't let their unbelief limit what you believe.

13.3   Don't Doubt—It Is Costly

What.You.Say.Is.What.You.Get. (WYSWYG)

After the king had validated the news that Samaria was delivered from the seige of the enemy through the lepers, he called a press conference and announced to the citizens that the recession was over, and there was plenty of food for everyone. He also announced that his right-hand officer, the same officer who doubted the prophecy about plenty, would oversee the food distribution program and maintain order.

When the people heard the news that there was food, they immediately and aggressively marched toward the city gate to enter the camp of the Syrians. The unbelieving officer stood at the gate trying to maintain order, but the mob was so desperate that they trampled him and he died on the spot. If you remember, the prophet had told him that he would see the miracle happen with his own eyes but would not be able to eat any of it.

If you want to see your life change dramatically, you will have to raise your belief level. Doubt is very costly! The prophet believed that the economy in Samaria would change for the better in twenty-four hours and it happened. The officer, on the contrary, believed that their economic situation could not change and he died (I guess) to prevent him from benefiting from what he did not believe.

> *I know it's easy for anybody to just fill in the blanks in section 13.1, or answer "No" to all the statements in section 13.2., but if you read any of the statements and doubt in your heart, it will not happen. Review your response to sections 13.1. and 13.2. above. If you doubt any of the "I believe . . ." statements in section 13.1 or think any of the statements in section 13.2 seem too good to be true, what makes you have such doubts? Be very honest:*

_____

_____

_____

> *Sometimes we doubt what we cannot yet see (faith) because of what we have already seen (fear). If this is the case with you, I suggest that you put yourself in an environment where you can constantly feed your faith and starve your fear.*

You cannot be in charge of what you don't believe. The officer on whose arm the king leaned was put in charge of what he did not believe, but he could not survive it. Whatever you want to do, whatever you want to become, wherever you want to go, if you think you can, you are right. If you think you can't, you are not wrong. If you are not going to die sitting, you need to believe in God and believe in yourself. Don't doubt, because unbelief will cost you.

ADD WORK

"You cannot fold your hands and allow weeds to grow in the garden of your life."

— Ghandi Olaoye

*Before you begin: Please familiarize yourself with **Chapter 14** of Don't Die Sitting, pp. 143–150.*

Many people have been handicapped by their faith. Billions of religious people are sending prayers to God in heaven while they refuse to take any action here on earth. Friend, nothing works until you work. The four men brought change to their city, not only because they have faith but also because they swung their feeble selves into action.

14.1   Nothing Works Until You Work

"My Father never stops working, and so I keep working too."

— Jesus Christ

You will read on pages 144–145 of **Don't Die Sitting** that the patriarchs were not only devout worshipers but also hardworking. All of them served God, but their allegiance to God did not replace their responsibilities to work. Besides, God was introduced to us in Creation as a Worker; Jesus came to this world to do the work of salvation. When Jesus left, the Holy Spirit continued the work in those who believe.

The problem today is that many lazy people use religion as crutches for limping through life.

If you are very religious and also very broke, you might want to check your work ethic. A wise man once walked by the field of a lazy person. He saw the field covered with weeds, overgrown with thorns, and surrounded by broken walls. The wise man thought about what he saw and concluded that the lazy man was poor because of negligence, extra sleep, and an "it-doesn't-matter" attitude about his business.

I want you to reflect on your field—your life, your family, your finances, your organization, your company, your career, or your business. Do you like what you see? Does it look like your field is uncultivated due to a bad work ethic, procrastination, or just neglect? What can you begin to do to cultivate your fields so that they are not taken over by weeds?

_____

_____

_____

_____

_____

14.2   You Were Born to Do Great Works

Going to work is not the same thing as working.

You cannot do great work with a lazy mind. You can be the light of the world, but darkness will take over your surrounding if you are not switched on. If you want to live a legacy, now is the time to get up, go out, put all you've got into what you want your legacy to be, and just do it. As the Good Book says, "Whatever your hand finds to do, do it with all your ability." Don't just go to work, do the work.

If you are not going to die sitting, you must be willing to do whatever it takes to make your impact. You can't give up easily and you can't let what you are going through stop you from where you are going to. What greater works have you imagined to do? I know you have dreams and aspirations, but I want you to write down one dream that really scares you.

_____

_____

_____

14.3   Prophecy Will Not Fulfill Itself

Like a bank check that is never cashed or a blueprint that never becomes a house, many people die with unfulfilled visions and unrealized dreams. That's because fulfilling prophecy does not take magic—it takes work.

In his famous "I have a dream" speech, Dr. Martin Luther King, Jr. dreamed of an America where people would "not be judged by the color of their skin, but by the content of their character." Dr. King prophesied that black men and white men, Jews and Gentiles, Protestants and Catholics would be able to join hands." Two years before Dr. King delivered his famous speech, Barack Obama was born. Although Obama might not have heard the live presentation of Dr. King's speech, he worked hard through school, as a community organizer, a fund-raiser, and a senator. He was bold enough to announce his candidacy for president of the United States. Although he was relatively unknown nationally when he began his bid for the White House, his oratory skills, his likeability, and—I believe—the Lord Factor led to his victory as the first African American to be elected president of the United States. This happened forty-six years after Dr. King's moving speech.

As Dr. King predicted, most Americans did not judge Obama by the color of his skin. Black and white, Catholics and Protestants, young and old, students and workers, immigrants and natives, and volunteers and paid staff worked together, prayed together, and struggled together to elect Barack Obama the forty-fourth president of the United States of America.

President Obama studied, worked hard, and persevered until he became the fulfillment to a prophecy that preceded him by forty-six years. The president did not just sit in Chicago wishing for the Oval Office in Washington, D.C. He worked hard to get there.

Have you at any time caught a glimpse of your future? Have you seen your future in a dream? Has anyone told you that you are going to be great, wealthy, or impact a lot of people? Do you look at someone great today and think to yourself: "That will be me in a few years"? If you answer yes to any of these (or similar) questions, congratulations! But there is work to do.

Since who you spend your time with and what you spend your money on have a huge impact on where you will end up in the near future. How will you rate yourself on these three questions—from 1 (Not at all likely) to 10 (Very likely)?

My bank account shows that I invest my money on activities and resources that will help me get to the future I see.

1   2   3   4   5   6   7   8   9   10

My calendar shows that I invest my time in places and with people who can help me get to the future I see.

1   2   3   4   5   6   7   8   9   10

My phone records show that I invest my time talking to people who can help me achieve my goals.

1	2	3	4	5	6	7	8	9	10

If you rate yourself 7 or less on any of these questions, it might be necessary to re-prioritize what you spend money on, where you spend your time, and the people you have on the front row of your life.

14.4   It's Your Time, and It's Your Turn

Now that you've been inspired to not die sitting, what are you going to do with the life you have left? Are you willing to do whatever it takes to get to your desired destination? You might lose some things on the way, but I have learned that what you will lose is nothing compared with what you will gain. In the end, you will look back and say, "It was worth it."

Like the sick lepers who ignored their own difficulties and chose their future because their past and their present had nothing to offer them, you, too, can bring deliverance to your situation, your family, your community, your state, and your country. But you will only be able to do it if you decide not to just sit there wishing for a change.

I am confident that this is your defining moment. This is your time to win! Now is your turn to shine! This is your season! I will see you at the top. Till then, I pray you will not die—sitting on the seed of greatness inside of you.

Congratulations! You have completed this study guide. Now that you have decided not to die sitting on your potential, take some time to reflect on your answers to the questions in this study guide, and write down three immediate actions you are going to take starting tomorrow.

Starting tomorrow, I will:

1. _____

_____

2. _____

_____

3. _____

_____

ABOUT THE AUTHOR

Saji Ijiyemi applies the principle in this workbook to individuals, small groups, entrepreneurs, small business, and corporate organizations, showing them how to use these principles and other life tools to discover and develop their core talents, inspire their team, and get results.

Speaking: Saji is in demand internationally as a speaker on the topics of leadership, team building, peak performance, personal growth, and spiritual growth. He is affiliated with the John Maxwell Team and speaks to individual groups, churches, and companies.

Individual and Group and Coaching: When working with you one-on-one, Saji's highest purpose is to help you discover your purpose and develop your potential. When working with a group, he empowers each person in the group to develop the leader within and shine in a safe environment that nurtures the group as a whole.

Training, Workshop, and Seminars: Saji also offers Half- or Full-day Workshops/Seminars, customized "Lunch and Learn," Keynote Speech for Your events, and In-House Corporate Training. Every year, he hosts Leadercast Baltimore, a one-day leadership simulcast that brings business and community leaders together.

Books: Saji Ijiyemi is a best-selling author whose books have inspired thousands of people around the world. His titles include *Don't Die Sitting* and the companion study guide, *How To Know Where You Fit in Life*, and many others are in the works.

For more information, please visit Saji at:

www.sajigroup.com or call +1 (240) 205-3074

ACKNOWLEDGMENTS

This companion study guide to Don't Die Sitting was made possible with help from my family and friends:

Miranda, thank you being my Chief Encouragement Officer. Besides taking care of me and the children, you made time to proofread, edit, answer the test questions in this workbook, and constantly suggests ways to make it more interactive. I know God was thinking of me when He made you.

To my talented children, princess Deborah and princes Ezra and Jesse, thank you for allowing me time to sit down, reflect, and re-examine my priorities as a dad. You have taught me to ask better questions.

To Pastor Lewis Lee, thank you for believing in me and for taking time to review this study guide.

To my friends and mastermind team: Abiola Saba, Tosin Olopade, Derric Yuh Ndim, Anthonia Ngafor, and Emmanuel Adegbola, this workbook was possible because of your invaluable contributions. Thank you very much.

To you, my friend, for taking the time to reflect on your life and your priorities. I dare you to take action every day to truly live while you are alive.

To all who are physically limited, but mentally limitless, thank you for constantly reminding us that what we have is more than what we lack.

CONNECT WITH SAJI

Wherever you are on social media, Saji is there. I'd like to connect with you, learn more about your life journey, and how I could help you achieve your goals. Here is how to find me online:

f	www.facebook.com/sajigroup
🐦	www.twitter.com/sajigroup
in	www.linkedin.com/in/sajigroup
g+	www.google.com/+sajigroup
▶	www.youtube.com/sajigroup
📷	http://instagram.com/sajigroup
P	www.pinterest.com/sajigroup
🔄	www.sajigroup.com

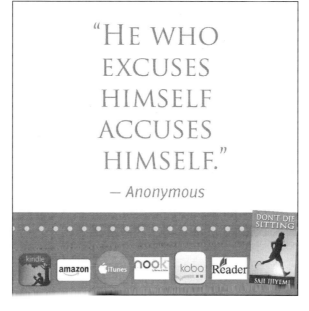

"HE WHO EXCUSES HIMSELF ACCUSES HIMSELF."

— *Anonymous*

NOTES